Endangered Animals

by Beth Parlikar

Editorial Offices: Glenview, Illinois • Parsippany, New Jersey • New York, New York
Sales Offices: Needham, Massachusetts • Duluth, Georgia • Glenview, Illinois
Coppell, Texas • Ontario, California • Mesa, Arizona

Every effort has been made to secure permission and provide appropriate credit for photographic material. The publisher deeply regrets any omission and pledges to correct errors called to its attention in subsequent editions.

Unless otherwise acknowledged, all photographs are the property of Scott Foresman, a division of Pearson Education.

Photo locators denoted as follows: Top (T), Center (C), Bottom (B), Left (L), Right (R), Background (Bkgd)

Opener: Digital Vision; 1 Digital Vision; 3 (CL, BL) Brand X Pictures; 3 (BR, CR) Digital Vision; 3 (C) Getty Images; 4 Digital Vision; 6 Medioimages; 7 Digital Vision; 8 (L) Getty Images; 9 Digital Vision; 10 Getty Images; 11 Ken Cole/Animals Animals/Earth Scenes; 12 Getty Images; 13 Willard Luce/Animals Animals/Earth Scenes; 14 Digital Vision; 15 ©Royalty-Free/Corbis; 16 Brand X Pictures; 17 Digital Vision; 18 Farrell Grehan/Photo Researchers, Inc.; 19 Getty Images

ISBN: 0-328-13526-7

Copyright © Pearson Education, Inc.

All Rights Reserved. Printed in the United States of America. This publication is protected by Copyright, and permission should be obtained from the publisher prior to any prohibited reproduction, storage in a retrieval system, or transmission in any form by any means, electronic, mechanical, photocopying, recording, or likewise. For information regarding permission(s), write to: Permissions Department, Scott Foresman, 1900 East Lake Avenue, Glenview, Illinois 60025.

3 4 5 6 7 8 9 10 V0G1 14 13 12 11 10 09 08 07 06

How many kinds of animals can you name? Of course you can name the easy ones, like dogs, frogs, whales, and snails. But it would take you a *very* long time to name them all. How long? Most scientists believe that there are at least three million species of animals. Some scientists think there may be as many as *one hundred million* species!

This variety of life is important for keeping our planet healthy. All species contribute to our planet's health by interacting with other species.

When all the members of a species die, that species becomes extinct. Many species have become extinct due to natural causes.

Humans sometimes cause animals to become extinct. People hunt some animals for food. They kill other animals because they are pests. Lions and bears are sometimes killed because people think they are dangerous. People also kill animals accidentally when they make changes to the **environment** where animals live.

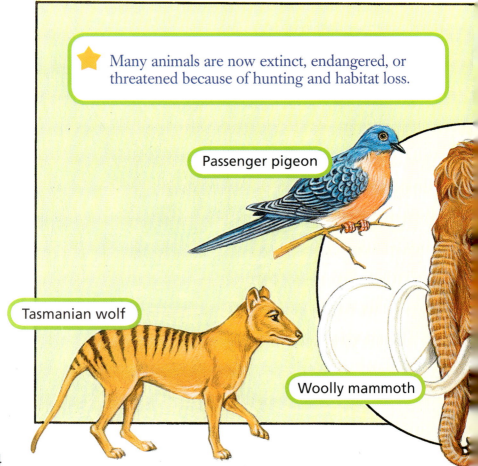

Many animals are now extinct, endangered, or threatened because of hunting and habitat loss.

Passenger pigeon

Tasmanian wolf

Woolly mammoth

Many species have already become extinct because of people's actions. Other species have very few members left and are in danger of becoming extinct. These species are called endangered species. Species that are close to becoming endangered are called threatened.

It is harmful to Earth's biodiversity when too many species become extinct, endangered, and threatened. The loss of so many different species upsets the balance of life on Earth.

Stellars sea cow

Giant moa

Dodo bird

In the United States, a law called the Endangered Species Act protects species that are in danger of becoming extinct. This law requires the government to list endangered species of animals and plants.

The law also requires that plans be made to keep these species from becoming extinct. These plans can include efforts to protect the habitats of endangered species. They might also call for the breeding of young animals in captivity.

Sometimes people lose their jobs or businesses because of these plans. Because of this not everyone agrees with the Endangered Species Act.

⭐ Overfishing has endangered many species of fish.

When humans change the environment, animals' homes are often destroyed. These animals must try to find new homes. Sometimes they can find a new place to live. But other times there is not enough space or food for them.

Animals that lose their homes are at much greater risk of becoming endangered or extinct. If we can prevent the loss of animals' homes, then they will have a much better chance of surviving. The best way to do this is by not allowing people to change the environments that animals live in.

Conservation of forests and other habitats helps to save endangered species.

One animal that has become endangered because of habitat loss is the giant panda. Giant pandas live in the forests of China.

Giant pandas weigh about two hundred pounds. They need to eat up to eighty-three pounds of bamboo every day! But many of China's bamboo forests have been cut down. This has made it very difficult for giant pandas to find food. At one time giant pandas were found in many parts of China. Now they live in only a few small patches of mountain forests.

Giant pandas used to be found throughout southeastern China. Today they live in only a few small areas.

- Present day China
- Historic range for pandas
- Current panda habitat

China

The hunting of giant pandas has also lowered their numbers. Giant pandas were hunted for their fur or captured illegally.

Today, scientists in China and the United States are working together to protect China's last remaining wild pandas. By working together, these scientists are achieving more than they could if they worked alone. One of their most impressive achievements happened in 1999 at the San Diego Zoo. Scientists there helped a pair of giant pandas give birth to a giant panda. It was the first healthy giant panda to be born in the United States!

Giant pandas are vegetarians. Their favorite food is bamboo.

The northern spotted owl is also threatened because of the loss of its forest home. This owl lives in the northwestern United States. More than 80 percent of the spotted owl's forests have been cut down for wood.

This small bird became famous when the federal government ordered logging companies to stop cutting down its forests. The spotted owl has a far better chance to survive now that its forests have been protected.

Northern spotted owls stay near the ground during the summer. They move to the treetops during the winter.

Small animals can be hurt by habitat loss as well. One example is the Karner blue butterfly. This beautiful insect once lived throughout the northeastern United States.

The caterpillars that become Karner blue butterflies eat wild lupine. People have changed the environment in a way that has caused wild lupine to stop growing. Now the caterpillars have nothing to eat. As a result the Karner blue butterflies have almost disappeared.

Some states are working to restore the wild lupine. The Karner blue butterflies are also being bred in zoos for release into the wild.

Karner blue butterflies are in danger due to the disappearance of wild lupine.

Hunting and fishing are important ways that people get food. But sometimes people hunt animals not for food but so they can sell the animals' body parts to other people. Illegal hunting or fishing is called poaching. It can cause animals to become endangered.

The rhinoceros is now almost extinct because of poaching. Poachers sell rhinoceros horns to people who use them as medicine. Governments have made great efforts to stop rhinoceros poaching. But the rhinoceros is still endangered.

Black and white rhinos look very similar. Black rhinos eat tree leaves and shrubs. White rhinos (like the ones shown below) eat grass.

Trumpeter swans live in North America. They are named for the loud calls they make while migrating.

Trumpeter swans were also hunted until they were almost extinct. Early American settlers hunted them for their long feathers. They used the feathers to make quill pens; later the feathers were used to decorate ladies' hats.

Scientists are now raising trumpeter swans in captivity. Their habitats are also being protected. As a result trumpeter swans have started to recover. They are no longer close to extinction.

⭐ The trumpeter swan is the largest water bird in North America.

Overfishing threatens many species of fish. The Atlantic salmon is especially threatened by overfishing. These fish hatch and grow up in rivers. Then they swim to the ocean. They live in the ocean for one or more years. When adult Atlantic salmon are ready to give birth, they return to the river they were born in. There they lay eggs.

Because of overfishing, fewer adult Atlantic salmon make it back to their rivers. In some rivers they have already become extinct. Atlantic salmon also become sick from pollution in the rivers and oceans. This makes it difficult for them to make the trip home.

Atlantic salmon may swim thousands of miles while traveling between the ocean and the rivers they grew up in.

Another animal that has been hurt by pollution is the manatee. Manatees are mammals. They are closely related to elephants. Manatees live in the warm rivers of the southeastern United States. They also live in the rivers of Central America and South America.

Pollution kills the underwater plants that manatees eat. Manatees are also hurt by motorboats. People who care about manatees are **enthusiastic** about cleaning up their habitat and preventing boats and pollution from hurting them.

⭐ Manatees are often injured or killed in collisions with speedboats.

The peregrine falcon is in less trouble than the manatee and Atlantic salmon. The story of its comeback is very encouraging.

Peregrine falcons became endangered because of a chemical in the environment. The chemical hurt their eggshells. Because of this their chicks were not able to survive. The number of peregrine falcons was greatly reduced.

Scientists bred peregrine falcon chicks in captivity and released them into the wild. The chemical that hurt their shells was also made illegal. As a result there are many more peregrine falcons alive today and they are no longer considered endangered.

⭐ Peregrine falcons are the fastest birds on Earth. They like to nest on cliffs or around tall buildings.

The red-legged tree frog, like other animals described in this book, has become threatened for several reasons. It is the most common frog in California.

These frogs were hunted for food. Many also died when their streams became polluted.

Bullfrogs have also hurt the red-legged tree frog. At some point bullfrogs were introduced to California. They ate so many red-legged tree frogs that they almost made them extinct.

The government has tried to help by setting aside land for the red-legged tree frogs. The frogs are given more protection on this land.

The red-legged tree frog was almost made extinct by bullfrogs.

Plants, like animals, can become endangered. The United States has more endangered plants than endangered animals.

The green pitcher plant lives in the southeastern United States. It gets its food by trapping insects. The green pitcher plant "eats" them by absorbing nutrients from their bodies.

The green pitcher plant has become endangered because of habitat loss. Scientists are now making an **investigation** into how we can save these endangered plants.

The green pitcher plant lives in the southeastern United States. Most of its habitat has disappeared.

What can you do to contribute to the protection of endangered species? More than you think!

You can begin by learning more about the endangered species in your area. Perhaps you could write an article for your school newspaper to educate others about what you've learned. Or maybe you can volunteer to clean up places in your community that have become polluted.

Whatever you choose to do can help our planet's endangered plants and animals. So start today in order to help protect life on planet Earth!

By writing a newspaper article about a threatened or endangered species, you can help life on our planet!

Glossary

conservation *n.* preservation from harm or decay.

contribute *v.* to help bring about.

enthusiastic *adj.* full of enthusiasm; eagerly interested.

environment *n.* conditions of air, water, and soil.

investigation *n.* a careful search.